Table of Contents

Rourke Educational Media

rourkeeducationalmedia.com

Can you find these words?

cicadas

crickets

mice

whales

Animals that Sing

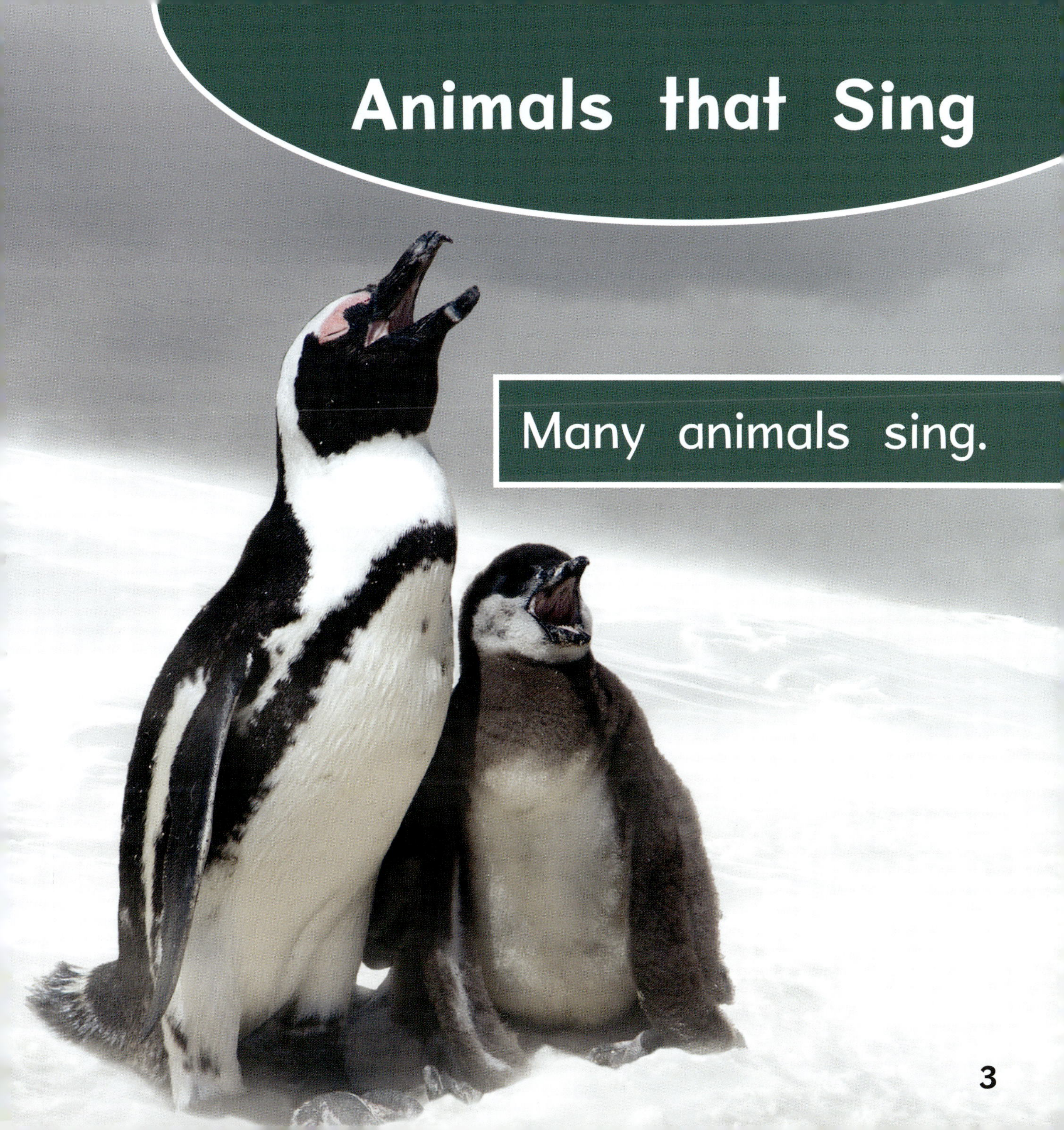

Many animals sing.

Birds sing to find mates.

They sing to say, "This is my space!"

Whales sing in the ocean.

They talk to other whales with their songs.

Crickets sing.

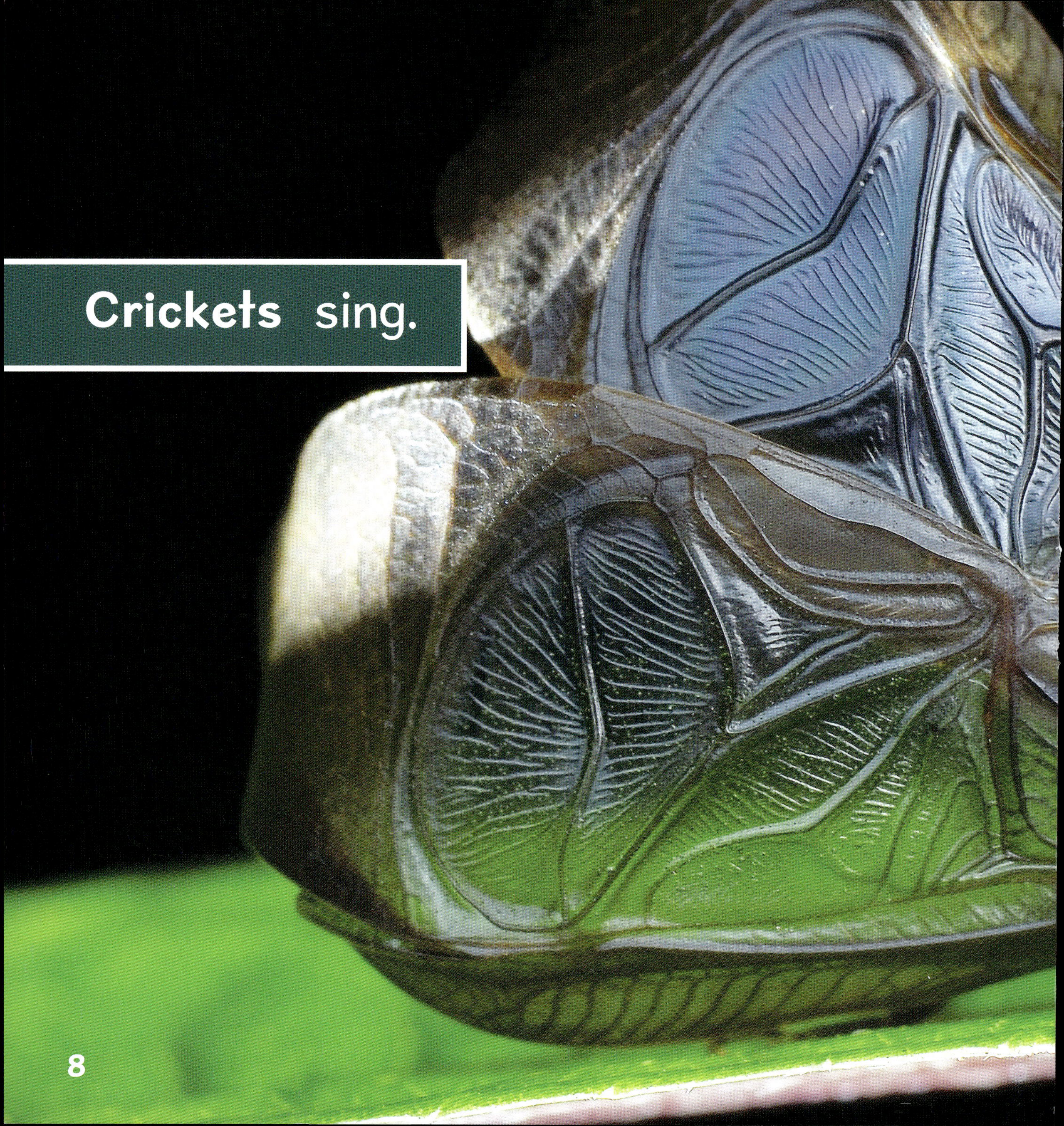

They rub their wings together to sing. Chirp, chirp!

Mice sing to find mates.
They sing to protect their homes.

Their songs are too high for human ears.

Cicadas sing. They sing loud!

They sing to keep birds away.

Did you find these words?

Cicadas sing. They sing loud!

Crickets sing. They rub their wings together to sing.

Mice sing to find mates.

Whales sing in the ocean.

Photo Glossary

cicadas (se-KA-das): Large insects that live most of their lives underground.

crickets (KRIK-its): Small insects in the grasshopper family.

mice (mise): Small types of rodents.

whales (wales): Huge mammals that live in the ocean.

Index

About the Author

Lori Mortensen lives in Northern California with her family and her cat, Max. When she's not tapping away at her computer, she likes to go bird watching and listen to the great-tailed grackles sing.

www.rourkeeducationalmedia.com

PHOTO CREDITS: Cover: Ken Canning; p.2,12,14,15: © emptyclouds; p. 2,8,14,15: © SIMON SHIM; p. 2,10,14,15: © CreativeNature_nl; p. 2,6,14,15: CoreyFord; p. 3: © Richmatts; p. 4: © Zwilling330

Edited by: Keli Sipperley
Cover design by: Kathy Walsh
Interior design by: Rhea Magaro-Wallace

Library of Congress PCN Data
Animals That Sing / Lori Mortensen
(Let's Learn)
ISBN (hard cover)(alk. paper) 978-1-64156-163-1
ISBN (soft cover) 978-1-64156-219-5
ISBN (e-Book) 978-1-64156-273-7
Library of Congress Control Number: 2017957774

Printed in the United States of America, North Mankato, Minnesota